MW00928044

TOTUMLUX

Awaken Your Light Body
with Nine New Words

RAYA ALEXANDER

All rights reserved

The characters and events portrayed in this book are fictitious. Any similarity to real persons, living or dead, is coincidental and not intended by the author.

No part of this book may be reproduced, or stored in a retrieval system, or transmitted in any form or by any means, electronic, mechanical, photocopying, recording, or otherwise, without express written permission of the publisher.

For more information, please visit:

www.rayaalexander.com.

Illustrations by: Benjavisa Ruangvaree

Library of Congress Control Number:

Printed in the United States of America

ISBN: 9798324797553

CONTENTS

1

INTRODUCTION

I've been blessed with amazing and often unexpected spiritual experiences throughout my life. In my twenties, one such experience was learning how to communicate with my Higher Self and spirit guides, the latter sometimes being called channeling. The key to learning this skill is discerning the frequencies of our own thoughts, versus the frequencies of more subtle thought forms and communications that are coming to us from the Beings of Light that can help guide us on our path. We have many helpers, teachers, healers, and loved ones who wish to see us thrive during our time here on Earth, and grow in line with our particular purpose for being here.

I had learned this skill from a friend of mine and practiced it often to get my soul's and angels' perspective on certain situations or questions. And while I went so far as to offer some small classes to teach people how to have these subtle conversations themselves, eventually life became too busy to stay in practice; I got married, had children, and grew a career. Some twenty plus years later, when life slowed down due to the Covid pandemic, I got back into the formal practice and remembered how nourishing it was on an internal level.

About a year or two into my renewed practice, I received messages from spirit advising me to study some Native American languages, particularly how they described spiritual concepts that were unique to their cultures. At the end I asked for the name of the spirit, he said Sequoyah. Later when I looked up Sequoia Native American (I spelled it like the tree) I found that Sequoyah was the name of a Cherokee Tribe member who had codified their tribe's language so that it could be written down. This was in the early 1800's before most of the indigenous North American tribes had written languages. Sequoyah himself didn't know how to read or write, so he started from scratch. This written language became a major support to the continuation of Cherokee culture and identity and in 1847 the massive Sequoia tree was named after him.

I then did some research on the spiritual concepts in the Cherokee language as well as in other Native American languages that had since found their way into the written word. The reason for this advice became clear to me. It was not so much to learn Native American languages, but to think about creating language for the spiritual light that I perceived while working with people.

As someone who works with energy and light in energy healing sessions, and also uses aura photography to help people see themselves as a being of light, I have become aware of many nuances about the light around us and inside of us. I started naming these distinctions specific words with Latin and Greek roots to make them sound and feel natural in our Western tongue. I feel using these words that have the same roots as the majority of the language we use every day helps to heal the split that we have in our culture between the material and spiritual realms. Becoming aware of ourselves as beings of light requires nuanced language that exists in ancient cultures such as India and China, but is limited in our Western culture. If we're made of light then we need more specific language to describe this light to help us become aware of it and what it's good for. Nuanced language creates more capacity to perceive things with our conscious mind, helping us to be more masterful in our environment and in life.

The first distinction of light, Totumlux, resonated closely with descriptions of the primal animating life force in ancient sacred texts. Hinduism calls it Purusha (pure consciousness), or refers to it with the phrase "not this, not that" to describe how undefinable it is! The foundational principal of Tao in Taoism is also considered to be un-describable, yet discernable through our intuition.

My goal in choosing what aspects to name was to keep it as simple as possible while still being specific. Just knowing a bunch of new words won't help anyone, but having an understanding that leads to an experience of these aspects of our light is transformational. At least, that is the experience for myself and my hope for you.

I'm a big believer in balanced left/right brain learning, and this balance is reflected in the variety of material in this book. In Part I we will explore these words, how they are interrelated with each other, as well as the significance they have for our human existence. I've included spaces after each of these chapters for you to draw, journal or just take a moment to reflect on what these energies/ideas mean to you. How do they feel? Does a picture come to mind that you can scribble out with stick figures, or something more elaborate if that is fun for you? Or are there some words you can jot down? Let these impressions flow freely with creative license to activate your right brain participation.

Part II is a fairy tale narrative that illustrates these terms using them creatively as characters and settings, making them easier to absorb. Part III is a guided meditation to help you experience these energies in a deeper more direct way. And lastly, the word definitions including their Latin and Greek roots are listed at the end of the book.

Now, to begin, the first and most critical distinction is that between Totumlux and Partiolux, the two fundamental aspects of energy sustaining us here on Earth.

PART I
Light Language

2

TOTUMLUX AND PARTIOLUX

You are made of energy. You are made of light. You are part of a massive, energetic system that exists to sustain you. The most fundamental of all light energies is Totumlux, or total light.

Totumlux *is the total or complete light at the source of all of creation that doesn't break down over time. The most subtle and core aspect of our collective being, it exists with or without its counterpart and derivative light, Partiolux.*

Partiolux *is partial light, a derivative of Totumlux, and is the light that matter is made of, that is subject to deterioration.*

Totumlux is the background field of energy that gives rise to all Partiolux manifestations; our bodies, animals, plants, minerals, and anything made from these organic creations.

Culturally we are trained to see ourselves as individual beings, separate from everything else, working in a mechanical universe where we have to go out and get everything done. And while we *are* individual separate beings, we are also beings made of light moving in an energetic universe from which we are not separate. Experiencing the Totumlux aspect of our being helps us to be more in tune with everything; ourselves, other beings, and the workings of the universe.

In slowing down Totumlux to become Partiolux and create gross matter such as our bodies, or subtle matter such as our thoughts and feelings, Partiolux becomes vulnerable to breaking down. This is why everything here on Earth, including our body-mind, breaks down over time.

The dualistic nature of life on earth is that we are both sources of this whole light and the expressions of it at the same time. Identifying too much with our Partiolux manifestations creates pain and suffering when they inevitably break down. When we are aware that our Partiolux body/person is just a small part of our being, not the entirety, we handle its decline with more grace and less fear. We realize that while our Partiolux is always changing, our Totumlux remains constant, strong and bright.

Part of being here seems to be forgetting our Totumlux source and believing that we are the fragments. Even if we successfully keep ourselves from identifying with external things such as work, accomplishments and possessions, the identification with our body and mind is hard to see past. Even our thoughts and feelings are expressions of our unique Partiolux frequencies, much like a painting is an expression of the artist. They aren't however, the most essential "you".

Your core light body is a unique combination of Totumlux frequencies. No two people are alike, and this includes their particular frequency combinations. Totumlux is always shining and serving as a blueprint for our entire being: our physicality, our emotional make-up and mental brilliance. Like a blueprint for an amazing building, it's always in its original authentic state.

Our particular Totumlux light grid helps us attune to our wholeness and wellness, guiding the life force within us towards healing. Awareness of our Totumlux has two advantages. First, it supports its function as a beacon for Partiolux to align with its source code and original functionality. This is how our body and mind heals, whether it is a gradual or immediate process.

Another benefit of Totumlux awareness is to enjoy life more even as the Partiolux layers of our being gradually deteriorate as they eventually do. Over time we can feel like a collection of aches, pains and problems as we get older. Sole identification with Partiolux is called Microvita, or small life, and results in a sense of separation from the totality of one's being. Developing a sense of identification with our source light that is always one hundred percent whole and healthy gives us an uplifting alternative to the pure Partiolux experience of life.

Your particular Totumlux combination holds imprints of your unique talents, strengths and areas of challenge. As you gain a deeper understanding of your intrinsic light, your authentic self, it turns from being a blueprint to a map, revealing the purpose and direction that's grounded in your soul's blueprint. By sharing your distinctive light and talents with others, you contribute to the world in a uniquely meaningful way. By aligning with your Totumlux, you inspire and uplift others, creating a positive ripple effect in the world.

We will inevitably have pain and sorrow in this life as we identify with Partiolux, light fragments and derivatives. If we become aware of the distinction between our Totumlux essence and Partiolux manifestations, we suffer less and live in an increasingly harmonious state of Totumlux awareness while still animating our physical, mental and emotional Partiolux.

Keep in mind that Partiolux is not negative because it is derivative light that deteriorates. The relationship between timeless Totumlux and temporal Partiolux is essential to life. Totumlux is the foundation that enables Partiolux creation to exist and thrive. Partiolux is the tangible and subtle art of our being. It's a universal experience to lose awareness of Totumlux while we are here on Earth. This dynamic is called

Dimentina, the complete forgetting of our source light (as well as where we came from before we had a Partiolux body).

As color frequencies, Partiolux is expressed as all the colors of the rainbow as well as their combinations and muted derivatives. Totumlux in its subtlety is clear, pregnant with the potential for any wavelength of color to emerge.

By recognizing that we are made of energy and light, and that our manifest being is a Partiolux expression of our deeper Totumlux nature, we can begin to see ourselves as part of a larger energetic universe. You may have perceived these distinctions already in deep meditation when you sensed the space between you and your thoughts, your feelings, and your body. In this space, your eternal Totumlux awareness shines.

Partiolux

words*thoughts*sketches

Totumlux

words*thoughts*sketches

3

TERRALUX AND AERLUX: LIGHT OF THE EARTH AND SKY

Totumlux is the creative force behind the Partiolux that makes up the Earth and the Sky, and each has its own unique expression of it. Terralux is the unique light of the Earth, and Aerlux is the signature energy of the Sky.

Terralux *is the grounded and stable light of the earth element, representing stability, manifestation and practicality.*

The Earth provides us with primal energy that supports our denser light layers, our physical and emotional energies. It comes up and through our energy circuits that are closest to the Earth. This grounding light nourishes us and does not break down - it is Terralux, the light of the Earth. What does it mean to be grounded? What's in the

21

Earth that supports us? There's dirt, rocks, and minerals that resonate with the physicality of our body. This aspect of Terralux strengthens our container, our particles that are organized into physiological systems of muscles, bones, blood, and organs.

Water also flows both in and on the Earth. Rivers, lakes, oceans, and underground reservoirs pulsate with their liquid light. This aspect of Terralux strengthens our emotional energy - the flow of our feelings as they come and go, not meant to be stagnant, but flowing freely.

Your body is a magnet that attracts Terralux wherever you are, both indoors and outdoors. Any time you are in nature - whether it be deep in the woods or standing on a small piece of dirt somewhere obscure - Terralux flows through you, bringing a sense of stability and grounding. Indoors, your body is a channel for this light as it moves through the Partiolux of buildings and walls, helping us to be more present and focused on the tangible aspects of life.

Aerlux *is the subtle and gentle light of the air element, representing communication, visionary thinking, intuition, imagination and faith.*

The essential light of the sky, Aerlux, supports our upper circuitry with more ethereal and expansive light. This light nurtures our thoughts, communication, intuition, and faith. As with Terralux, Aerlux supports us both outdoors and indoors. Spending time under an open sky brings us a sense of expansiveness and openness, and our connection to the universe as a whole. Even taking a few deep breaths while indoors can clear our minds of old, repetitive mental energy, bringing greater clarity, creativity, and inspiration. Aerlux stimulates the subtle signals and messages of our intuition, our inner voice. Our deeper sense of meaning and purpose is made more conscious.

Red is the color frequency closest to the Earth and expresses Terralux with its grounding effect. The warm red of Terralux pulls us close to the Earth and helps us to secure what we need from it. Blue is the energy of Aerlux with its shorter wavelength that nourishes our subtle faculties. It is expansive and helps us to see a bigger picture in life.

Terralux and Aerlux connect us with the nourishing energies of the Earth and Sky. We need both of these light energies; Terralux to nourish our denser systems, and Aerlux to nourish more subtle aspects of our being. As we grow our appreciation of Aerlux and Terralux and the role they play in our lives, we develop a greater respect and reverence for the natural world and our place within it.

Terralux and Aerlux reach us from opposite directions, up from the Earth and down from the Sky, creating a pillar of light that moves through our core; up from the base of our spine and down from the top of our head. Moving through this channel, they meet in the middle; your spiritual heart.

Terralux

words*thoughts*sketches

Aerlux

words*thoughts*sketches

4

CORCANTI: OUR HEART LIGHT

Corcanti *is the transformative light of the spiritual heart, which creates balance, healing and unconditional love, and is created by the meeting of Terralux and Aerlux.*

Corcanti is the transformative light of the spiritual heart, which creates balance, healing and unconditional love, and is created by the meeting of Terralux and Aerlux.

Corcanti, the transformative light of the spiritual heart, is a beautiful fusion of Terralux and Aerlux, representing the meeting point of Earth and Sky energies within our being. This merging in the heart center creates a harmonious balance, akin to a dance between these two powerful forces, giving rise to Corcanti: the melody of the heart. This divine music not only embodies unconditional love but also carries healing frequencies that can restore and rejuvenate.

At its core, Corcanti resonates with the frequencies of

unconditional love, radiating compassion, gratitude, and abundance. It is a symphony of light that nurtures our relationships, fostering deep connections with our loved ones in an environment of acceptance and care. Forgiveness, a key component of Corcanti, allows us to release the shackles of the past, freeing up our energy to fully embrace the present moment and facilitate healing in our hearts, minds and bodies.

As a color frequency, Corcanti is green, which is in the middle of the visible light spectrum. Being in the middle is significant, as it is the most balanced of all the color frequencies and helps to create greater coherence and alignment throughout our Partiolux energy bodies. By harnessing the energies of both the Earth and the Sky, our heart becomes a wellspring of vitality and balance, facilitating holistic healing.

Try this now: Picture someone you care about deeply before you. Someone for whom you hold compassion and unconditional love. They might be a family member, friend, or a pet! As you picture them, pay attention to what is occurring in your heart. Do you feel any energy moving? It might feel like warmth, or even a bit of pressure as your heart opens. This is the music of Corcanti, your heart strings being played.

Now, experiment with sending Corcanti to someone that you have some conflict with, maybe someone that you have been hurt by. See them before you, feel what is happening in your heart center. Does it feel tighter? Not as open? Relax your mind and take a deep breath. Feel or see Aerlux flowing through you from above, and Terralux rising up through your core from below. Allow your heart to become full, and without analysis or striving, simply allow these energies to flow to this person from your heart and surround them. How does this feel? See if simply sharing the light that flows through you allows for some compassion and subtle healing to take place.

Corcanti emanates from the center of our being, our heart center, and is expressed through the color green which is in the middle or center of the visible light spectrum. Being in the middle is significant, it is the most balanced of all the frequencies making it restorative, healing and rejuvenating for our equilibrium.

In observing the natural world, we can see the manifestation of Corcanti in the growth of trees, crops, and flowers. These earthly beings draw nourishment from both the soil and the sky, absorbing the energies required for growth and fruition. While the fruits of crops come in a rainbow of colors, the plants that grow them are typically green. These plants act as a natural conduit for Corcanti, supplying us with all the nutrients and colors that we need for nourishment. Consuming these fruits sustains our Partiolux bodies and revitalizes our Totumlux vibrancy.

Gratitude is a potent energizer of Corcanti, amplifying its healing and loving qualities. When we practice gratitude, we acknowledge and appreciate the abundance that surrounds us, anchoring ourselves in the present moment. Similar to forgiveness, gratitude shifts our focus from the past to the present, allowing us to fully engage with the healing and loving energies of Corcanti.

In essence, Corcanti is a profound expression of the interconnectedness of all things, a reminder of the harmonious dance between Earth and Sky within our hearts. It is a gentle yet potent force that can transform our lives, nurturing our souls and guiding us on a path of healing and unconditional love.

RAYA ALEXANDER

Corcanti

words*thoughts*sketches

5

AUTOGRATIS: SELF-LOVE

Autogratis *is surrounding oneself in one's own Corcanti energy of unconditional love and compassion, accepting both the whole and the broken pieces.*

Autogratis, a term born from the essence of self-love and compassion, encapsulates the profound act of enveloping oneself in the boundless embrace of Corcanti energy. It's about acknowledging every facet of one's being, both the pristine and the fractured fragments, with an unwavering sense of acceptance and gratitude.

At its core, Autogratis draws from Totumlux, the eternal wellspring of unchanging light from which all existence emanates. It transcends the limiting mindset of Partiolux, which insists on fixing perceived flaws before embracing self-love. Instead, Autogratis recognizes the inherent dualistic nature of existence, embracing both the well-developed aspects and the broken pieces with tender compassion.

Embracing Autogratis means embracing yourself wholly, flaws and all, while nurturing compassion for the journey of self-discovery and growth. It stands in stark contrast to the harsh voices of self-criticism and judgment, nurturing the harmonious flow of Corcanti, the symphony of the heart, towards oneself. This practice serves as a potent healing elixir, soothing the wounds and scars of self-rejection and denial. As each fragmented aspect of the self is bathed in the light of self-love and acceptance, it finds solace and integration within one's being.

Gratitude becomes the amplifier of Autogratis, reclaiming energy once entangled in the web of negative self-talk and criticism. By fostering gratitude for oneself, one unlocks the flow of Corcanti for healing, rejuvenation, and a profound sense of wholeness.

However, embracing Autogratis does not imply complacency. True transformation arises from acceptance rather than rejection. An example of this is relating to our bodies. We feel fat, and we turn this feeling into something that is wrong with us and that we must fix. However the key element to sustained personal change is acceptance. This would be acceptance of, for example, our belly; its size, shape and heaviness. How it has stored energy for us, and how it is unique to us.

This embracing of our present state of being gathers

our energy from the past (pining for how we used to look) and the future (wishing for a flatter stomach) and allows us to fully experience our stomach right now without judgment or criticism. This state of inner nurturance fuels positive choices from a place of less stress. We then naturally make food choices that match this inner sense of well-being more and more often.

The signature frequency of Autogratis is the gentle hue of pink, softening the edges of self-perception and inviting gentle self-embrace. While the red of Terralux helps us to feel safe in the physical world, the pink of Autogratis nurtures emotional safety. This includes the space to fully experience and embrace all feelings, even those we tend to suppress due to societal expectations.

Allowing Autogratis to permeate every aspect of one's being—thoughts, feelings, and past actions—fosters a profound sense of wholeness and rootedness. It is in the practice of self-directed acceptance and gratitude that one truly embodies Autogratis, fostering a deep and enduring love affair with oneself. Through this expansive journey of self-love, one discovers the transformative power of embracing one's entirety with open arms, enriching not only one's own life but also the lives of those around them.

Autogratis

words*thoughts*sketches

6

PAXLIBRA: EXPERIENCE OF WHOLENESS AND BALANCE

Paxlibra *is luxuriating in the experience of wholeness coming from the awareness and balance of these light forces in and around you.*

Paxlibra is enjoying the awareness and play of Totumlux and Partiolux, of Aerlux and Terralux, and of Corcanti and Autogratis in your life. These frequencies run through your body and being with ease the more you are aware of them and clear the way for them.

When you're aware of Totumlux frequencies shining through Partiolux, you have one foot in the manifest and one in the unmanifest. You take yourself more Light-ly as you are cognizant of the powerful creative light at the source of everything. You are less attached to its infinite Partiolux creations, meaning everything that can be perceived with our physical senses. Respect for these creations, whether they be physical, emotional or mental expressions, is not diminished because they are made of the type of light that breaks down over time. Rather they can be even more appreciated for their temporal beauty and usefulness.

Sensing Totumlux frequencies in its particular forms of Terralux and Aerlux helps you to balance the needs of your gross and subtle bodies. Do you need some movement and good food to nourish your denser aspects? Maybe some contemplation or singing to strengthen your Aerlux flow? A person who is naturally more attuned to Aerlux might focus a bit more on strengthening Terralux flow, and vice versa.

The essence of Paxlibra is not a particular color, rather it is the unique blend of colors that make up a person's authentic light. Paxlibra is naturally experienced when Terralux and Aerlux course through you blending together in the center of your being. Paxlibra grows as you balance sharing Corcanti with others, and Autogratis with yourself. Your authentic light then shines more brightly, blossoming as your unique contribution to life and those around you.

In Paxlibra, the beauty and abundance of life are more present, you experience more harmony with the world around you, and more quiet within you. Luxuriating in Paxlibra brings deep peace and fulfillment.

Paxlibra

words*thoughts*sketches

7

GAINING TOTUMLUX AWARENESS

So all this begs the question of how to develop and sustain an awareness of Totumlux and all of its facets. This book so far has given you intellectual knowledge of them. Studying these descriptions will encourage understanding and appreciation for these forces.

This text is intentionally short so that sections may be read multiple times to saturate the conscious mind with these distinctions. Practicing this way could involve, for example, reading one section a day for a month.

The fairy tale in Part II will help your right brain to absorb these distinctions in an easy manner by being illustrated through characters, places and occurrences in the story.

Using the guided journey that is part III of this book

will bring you more experiential awareness of these elemental light forces. Repeating the journey as a practice will help develop awareness memory, like muscle memory, of Totumlux and its different expressions.

Once these distinctions of Totumlux are in your field of awareness, further growth will be had through contemplation of them during everyday activities. Try being aware of the light innervating your hands as you type, your food as you eat, and your car as you drive. Focusing on these types of things may sound too mundane to be a sacred practice, but since Totumlux is at the source of everything, all situations can be used for practice.

Various forms of meditation amplify Totumlux perception, whether they are still forms of meditation or more active ones, by creating more space between our thoughts where Totumlux is more easily perceived. With these practices, slowly but surely your consciousness will be infused with more and more Totumlux awareness that will nourish, uplift and transform your daily experience into Paxlibra, luxurious balance and wholeness.

In the realm of spiritual light, the paradox of effort arises as a subtle but important factor. Unlike the tangible world where exerting effort often yields results, the ethereal nature of spiritual light requires a different approach. Striving too intensely can hinder the delicate process of connecting with this subtle energy. It's akin to trying to grasp a whisper—effort disrupts the stillness required to perceive the nuances of our subtle realms. In contrast, a more gentle and receptive state, free from the rigidity of effort, allows us to attune ourselves to quiet frequencies. It's an art of letting go, of allowing rather than forcing—a surrender to the innate luminosity that unfolds when we release the need to actively seek, and instead simply be present in the quiet space where our spiritual light naturally resides.

PART II
Kingdom Totumlux

8

KINGDOM TOTUMLUX: THE JOURNEY OF CANTI AND STELLA

Totumlux Kingdom is a beautiful place to live made of liquid light that shapes itself instantly to whatever needs and desires one has. Create a thought, hold it for a moment, and bang! There it is. A house, a sandwich, a spaceship, anything one could think of shows up. On top of that, this land is a place where the feelings of love, harmony and wholeness are easily experienced.

The ruler of Totumlux, King Iris, had many children whom she loved and adored. She would carefully teach them how to create with the energy inherent to the realm. This special light contained all the frequencies of creation in it, and moved lightning fast to manifest whatever someone intended. While fun and wonderful, it could also be a problem, as one would briefly entertain the thought of an elephant in the room, and there would be an elephant in the room! Then they thought to make the room larger to accommodate the elephant, and suddenly the room was as big as a lake. And then, as long as there was more room, people thought up more and more animals into the giant room. So many days were spent either in a real zoo, or in a zoo-like atmosphere with voluminous and varied creations popping up every moment.

King Iris loved this time of creative playfulness with her children. At the same time she wanted them to learn to focus their creative power with more intentionality, so she decided to start sending the older ones to Partio Academy to learn to harness their creative power and light bending skills.

When it came time for her twins, Canti and Stella, to go away for school, Iris called them to her. She told them that they would be going to a school of slower frequencies known as Partio Academy. There they would learn to create and use light more slowly and carefully. The slower manner of Partiolux made it easier to learn how to shape, use, and enjoy light. Partio Academy had two campuses where different things were taught, one in Aerluxia and the other in Terraluxburg.

"Dimentina will bring you through the frequency portal to Partio Academy. She is new at this, and has not perfected the process, but it's quite safe. However it's likely that you'll forget about where you came from when you get there. So it might be a little disorienting, but over time try to remember," King Iris said to her beloved twins.

"Forget? I don't think so" said Stella.

"Well, don't worry, either way you will have many wonderful experiences exploring and enjoying this slower dimension of Partiolux, or partial light, that is used there." Dimentina arrived to take Canti and Stella to Partio Academy. Iris hugged her children and placed a blessing on their heads. "May you be happy and healthy. May you find joy, and peace, and wisdom in your travels, and may you stay deeply connected to your highest purpose for this journey." Canti and Stella gave their mother a quick hug and excitedly followed Dimentina out the door. "I hope they remember me," she said after they were gone.

Dimentina brought them to an octagonal room with high domed windows looking out onto the landscape of Totumlux Kingdom. There were only two colors that made everything up, white and clear. The mountains and valley and river were all various shades of these two colors, the only ones Canti had ever known.

Dimentina gave them white cloaks which were very heavy. "These will help you land and not float away since you are so much lighter than everything where we are going."

"Where's that?" Canti asked.

"Terraluxburg. We'll be there as soon as," Dimentina paused.

"As soon as …?" said Stella.

"I forget exactly, but soon." she replied. Canti and Stella stared out the windows as the landscape started to change. The many shades of white and clear started to get darker and change into vibrant tones, darker and richer than anything she had ever seen.

"What's happening?" Canti asked.

"Those are the colors of Terraluxburg. Red, orange and yellow," Dimentina explained. "See? The ground is deep red, the bushes and trees are shades of orange and the Sky, that's yellow."

Canti and Stella stared breathlessly. "This is so cool!" Stella exclaimed. Canti noticed the walls of the room also looked different. She reached out to touch a wall.

"That's gold," said Dimentina.

Dimentina brought them to meet Microvita, their new teacher. "Welcome to Terraluxburg, it's always a joy to have new students! Where do you hail from?" he queried. Canti and Stella looked at each other. They weren't sure. Dimentina jumped in. "Same place they all come from, Microvita, you know that."

Microvita assured Canti and Stella, "No worries, there's so much to do here you probably would have forgotten your past anyway. Let me show you around."

Terraluxburg was a busy place full of many wonders. People were building houses and working in gardens. There was a large outdoor area where people were cooking and helping prepare the welcome feast. A group of students were practicing a dance for the evening's entertainment.

That night all the new arrivals were celebrated with delicious food, song, and dance. It came time for Microvita to address the new students. "Here at Terraluxburg you will learn about the energy of the Earth called Terralux and all the amazing things you can do with it. Explore and learn as much as you can, as your time here is limited. Tomorrow your basic training will begin!"

The next morning, Canti and Stella joined the other new students out in a field of golden grass. Canti stood by Stella in the back of the class. Ahead of them were dozens of other new students, all wearing heavy white cloaks. Microvita stood in front of the class on a small rise of land where they could all see him, and began to teach.

"Feel your feet inside your shoes and how they are distinct from one another, separate things, feet and shoes." After a long pause he continued, "Good, now feel your feet and your shoes as frequencies, vibrations. What is the vibration of your feet, your shoes? How about the Earth beneath your shoes? Can anyone feel that?" One person to the left of the group raised their hand. "Good. Softly, softly, welcome Terralux, the energy of the Earth." Microvita encouraged.

Canti saw something happening in that student's cape. Red, orange, and yellow hues at its hem were making their way slowly upwards. Canti looked at her own cape, which is still pure white. She closed her eyes.

"Open my feet softly," she said to herself as she relaxed her mind and focused on the sensations of her feet, her shoes, and the Earth beneath her. Then she felt a wave move through her. Startled, she looked down and saw faint warm colors starting to grow at the hem of her cape. "Stella, look!" she said.

When Stella didn't respond, she looked to see if they had heard her. To her surprise, Stella's entire cape was glowing with vibrant shades of red, burgundy, orange, peach, yellow, and gold. Despite its weight, their cape billowed around them slightly as they concentrated with eyes closed.

Feeling a bit jealous, a thought came to Canti's mind. "Don't compare yourself, it squashes your creative flow," advice she felt like she got when she was young (but she couldn't remember from whom).

Focusing once more, she inhaled and imagined herself drawing Terralux into her feet and legs, then let it spread to the rest of her body as she exhaled. She did feel calmer but still eager to see results. Her cape had color growing a few inches up from the bottom. She wasn't sure what made her think of focusing on breathing in the color and energy, but it seemed to be working.

Meanwhile, Microvita had been walking through the lines of the students observing their progress. Canti was trying hard to make her cape colors grow larger before he got to her, but this extra effort went awry, and all the colors drained out just as Microvita reached her. "Using the breath, good idea," he said to her. He then walked over to Stella, who was still quietly in their inner world connecting with Terralux, colors flying across their cape. Microvita smiled and then continued on, passing Stella by without a word.

That afternoon the students were given time to explore the different areas of learning available to them so they could choose what specific skills they would study while in Terraluxburg. The classes in Terraluxburg focused on tangible trades, oftentimes including how to use their hands to make things. Farming, construction, cooking, sewing, making medicines or jewelry were all things that both Canti and Stella could choose from.

Stella joined the team of students who were building houses. They worked hard and learned to use hand tools and all kinds of materials to build safe, strong houses. Stella loved being physical and feeling the weight of their body in Terraluxburg. They felt how their body got stronger when they used it, and how they could create something tangible and useful with their hands.

Canti was attracted to working in the garden. She learned how to grow vegetables and berries, and also herbs that had healing properties to replenish the body. The class spent time both outside working with nature, and inside cooking up what they had grown into delicious meals and healing tinctures. And each day she got to see Stella for the morning practice of connecting with Terralux. She got better and better at feeling this energy as she worked in the garden and in the kitchen and it was deeply satisfying.

As she spent more time working with plants and herbs, Canti started to see light coming from them. The plants appeared porous with clear light shining through invisible pores. "This light is so beautiful! It reminds me of something, but what?" Canti wondered. She told Stella about it, thinking that maybe because they were so good at running energy through their cape that they would be sensing this too. But Stella wasn't seeing it, and couldn't help her remember why it felt so familiar.

Microvita summoned Canti and Stella the next day. "You have done well here, and now it is time for you to move on to Aerluxia for new lessons." The three of them went back to the gold portal room. Once again the landscape outside the windows started to shift and became blurry, and then refocused with new colors. Canti was eager to know these new colors, and Microvita offered before being asked, "Now the Sky is blue, the Earth is indigo, and the trees are violet."

"And the walls?" Stella asked.

"Silver," Microvita replied. "Aerluxia is the school of the Sky energies. We'll follow the road up to the village where you can choose your studies."

Canti wondered why the portal brought them outside of the village rather than right to it, but she looked forward to the walk. Before long her senses attuned to the dynamic qualities of the Sky, how the sunlight danced among the tree leaves, and how the breeze cooled her skin. She heard birdsong welcoming her to Aerluxia. The simple enjoyment of these things made her cape glow with many different blues, purples and silver. She realized she was connected to Aerlux! And this time it was effortless.

Microvita brought them on a tour of the different study groups they could join. They saw people working with communication devices, people meditating, artists painting pictures, and rooms full of people talking about ideas. Stella joined a group of students who were creating designs for buildings, and Canti was drawn to a group who were learning a new language.

Stella became fascinated with architecture, how to dream up a building and create a blueprint for it. They had so many ideas for buildings that would serve so many different purposes. As they drew the designs from their imagination, shades of violet and indigo pulsed through their cloak.

Canti enjoyed learning to speak in different languages. As the group practiced speaking with each other, shades of blues and silver ran through their cloaks. Some days she would also see the clear light that she had been seeing in the plants coming from her friends and fellow students. It was subtle, and it made them seem softer and lighter. She was growing used to it, but she still wished she could remember what it reminded her of.

One of her classmates fell ill and was missing a lot of classes. Canti was sorry she had left her herbal tinctures in Terraluxburg, but decided to try using words as healing tools to see if she could help him feel better. She came to his bedside in the sick bay and told him a story where he was the main character. In this story, he went through trials and triumphs, and in the end experienced rejuvenation, healing and balance. The words were full of love and compassion, and they came to her mind as she focused on the clear light she saw coming from him. The words, ideas and feelings seemed to strengthen that light, and she spoke to him until his clear light radiated strongly and he felt better.

As she was finishing, she heard Microvita from behind her. "Look at your cloak." he said. Canti turned her focus to herself and saw some new colors running through her cape while he named them. "Those are shades of green and turquoise, along with silver and gold. Beautiful aren't they?"

Canti was amazed every time she saw new colors and this time was no different. "What land are they from?" she asked.

"These colors appear when the Aerlux and Terralux meet and blend in your spiritual heart. Here they create a

very balanced frequency that is healing and rejuvenating. They help you to play your heart song or Corcanti, the music of your love and compassion." said Microvita.

"So my name means song?" asked Canti.

"Yes, your mother sensed you would have a strong one when she named you. Now we see she was right!" Microvita said, revealing his pride in her.

Canti hoped he could answer the question that no one else seemed to be thinking about. "Microvita, do you see the clear light that shines from people and plants, and well, basically everything?"

"This is more of an advanced technique, but I'm not surprised that you are already aware of it. What you are seeing is Totumlux, the source of everything in these lands. Everything here in Partio Academy is made of denser light particles that are derived from this light. This denser light is called Partiolux," he replied.

"Am I supposed to do something with this… Totumlux?" asked Canti.

"Just sensing Totumlux, seeing it, feeling it or simply knowing that it's there, can be useful. Partiolux is beautiful but breaks down and eventually wears out, which is why everything in this land is temporary. Being aware of Totumlux can make things stronger, like you do when you tune into it to share your healing stories. Or it might just give us comfort with its constant light as we live in a continually changing world," Microvita explained.

Canti understood what he was talking about. Whenever she felt or saw this luminous quality around something or someone, she felt a sense of completeness and sometimes even transcendence. Everything was OK underneath it all, even when things were broken or in need of healing.

That night Corcanti burst into Stella's room. "I remember! The light that I'm seeing, I remember what it reminds me of. Home. Do you remember? Our mother is King Iris, and we lived with her in Totumlux Kingdom."

"Totumlux? Sounds cool, but no, I don't remember that." Stella responded. "But hey, check out my design for a village we're going to build." Stella showed her a large blueprint. "It's a group of homes connected to a central building where people can help each other with cooking and child care and sharing whatever special skills they have with each other."

As Stella spoke, Canti saw that their robe ran shades of blue and red with gold and silver highlights. The lively, vivid colors matched Stella's passion and enthusiasm for their project. Rather than interrupt them to point this out, she continued to watch and enjoy the unique combination of Aerlux and Terralux flowing through them.

Canti was requested more and more often at the sick

bay as people heard about her healing stories. She even started traveling back to Terraluxburg to help the patients there. She felt good that she could help so many people doing something that she loved. After a while though, she started to feel worn down, like she needed time off to restore herself. This was hard as she was the only one doing this type of service at the time. She was giving it so much effort that she was becoming out of balance and sick herself.

Canti thought about how she could tend to her own needs. She decided to tell herself a healing story in which she allowed others to help her and support her. In her story, other people learned how to tell the healing stories so she could be part of a team and share the workload. This story helped her to feel so much better that she decided she would recruit some helpers when she went back to work.

After her story for herself was done, she realized there was one more thing she did with her patients, which was to send them love and acceptance with her words and thoughts. So she took a deep breath and directed these feelings toward herself, unconditional love and deep self-acceptance. Being the receiver of her own self gratitude and acceptance felt awkward at first, but then she saw how it helped her, the same way it had helped others.

She went to tell Microvita of what she was learning about self-love. "You have hit upon a wonderful dynamic. What will you call it?" he asked.

Canti thought and listened for a few moments.

"Autograti, gratitude for myself." Upon saying this her cloak shimmered with emerald green sparkles!

"I think that will do nicely." Microvita said.

Both Stella and Canti's cloaks were now fully colored, and with particular brightness if they were sharing their Corcanti with others. They were ready to graduate. Microvita came to congratulate them. "You've done well. You've learned to sense and work with both Terralux and Aerlux, and mix the two into your special blend of Corcanti. I hope you have enjoyed your time here."

"It's over?" asked Stella.

"Your formal training taught you how to sense these energies, and now you can continue to learn from them directly," he replied.

"Do we stay here?" Canti asked.

"If you like," said Microvita. "You can also visit Totumlux Kingdom where you came from."

"Yes, I remember that place!" exclaimed Canti. "Back through the portal?"

"Anytime you wish to visit Totumlux, just remove your cape. But don't lose it, it holds the knowledge that you've gained here. You've worked hard on it," Microvita advised.

Canti untied the ribbon at the top of her cape. She carefully took it off and folded it over her arm. As she did, everything became very light. At first the light was so bright she couldn't see, but as her eyes adjusted she saw her mother, King Iris standing before her. She looked so different though! Before she saw her mother in shades of white and clear, just like all of Totumlux Kingdom. Now she could see the incredible colors of her kingly robes, and the darkness of her skin and hair. Canti sensed that these colors had been there all along, but she only learned to see them during her training.

She ran up and gave her mother a hug. She felt warmth oozing through her pores as she was hugged back. "Mother, I have so much to tell! You should see all of the places and people at Partio Academy. It's incredible!" Canti blurted.

"I know, I saw you and Stella at work when I came around to visit. You never really leave Totumlux, it just feels like that because Aerluxia and Terraluxburg are so much denser. Now you will be able to enjoy all three places as you have learned how to use the light frequencies that create them" the King said proudly.

"Should we ask Stella to come visit? Canti asked. "Their cape is so full of colors! They've decided to design and help build communities. They've come up with some amazing plans. But they don't remember you, or all this."

Smiling, her mother said, "That's okay, they're

enjoying life, they'll come visit when they're ready."

Canti settled in the land of Partiolux where she experienced the balance of energies blending from the Earth and the Sky. Most days she let her Corcanti flow to share healing and compassion with others. She also made sure to sing to herself in Autograti. Every day she tuned into Totumlux to remember her source and make sure she didn't identify too much with the changing world of Partiolux.

One day as she sat basking in the afternoon sunlight, she felt this balance and peacefulness must have a name as it was so sweet and transcendent. Just then, two words from her language studies flashed in her mind's eye; Pax and Libra. She remembered that Pax meant peace, and Libra meant balance. Paxlibra, the peace of balance. Balance between Aerlux and Terralux energies, balance between Totumlux and Partiolux awareness, and balance between sharing Corcanti with others and Autogratis with herself. She liked it and wrote it down.

PART III

Totumlux Meditation

9

TOTUMLUX MEDITATION

Take a few long, deep breaths, all the way down into your belly. As you inhale, breathe in ease and lightness. As you exhale, release any tension or holding that you become aware of. Good. You're going to dive into an experience of yourself as a being of light and the different layers of your light body. Everything about you is made of energy, including your physical body, which is the densest layer of your energy. We'll begin by bringing awareness fully into the body with a simple body scan and releasing any tension or holding that can easily be let go.

Starting at the top of your head, bring your awareness down into your face. See if you can relax your face just five percent more. Become aware of the tension held in the facial muscles and gently relax them. As you move through your body, look for areas of tension that can easily be let go, and allow this tension to get heavy and melt down towards the floor. Moving from your face to the back of your head, relax your scalp muscles. Then, down into your neck, relaxing the back of your neck, the front of your neck, allowing tension to get heavy and melt down into your chest. Open up your chest and relax.

Continue down into your belly. See if you can open up your belly and really let it decompress. Take a deep breath and feel how your belly rises and falls. Excellent. Now, move back up to your shoulder blades. Let them relax a bit more, and then melting down your back into your lower back. Let go of any tension that you sense there.

Move down into your hips and relax them. Notice if either butt cheek is tight and relax your hips and glutes, allow any tension to melt, get heavier, and then move down through your thighs, your knees, your calves, and finally, down through your feet. Good. Now send this ball of tension and holding down through the floor and into the earth, where it is absorbed, transformed, and released. Very good. Now, bring your awareness to your mental energy. Your mental energy is much more subtle than your physical energy and moves much more quickly. It spends a great deal of time in both the past and the future, as it's multidimensional. It often goes to the past to relive events, tweaking them to see if a different outcome would have been possible. Also reliving things you enjoyed, or things you didn't enjoy. Or it might go to the future, tweaking future events for optimization, things you're looking forward to, or things you're anxious about.

Your mind works incredibly hard throughout your life, all the learning and communication and navigation and decision-making, and the previewing and the reviewing. Take a moment to thank your mind for all of this incredible work it does for you throughout your life. Thank you, thank you, thank you.

Now, invite your mind to join you in the present moment. Ask it to relax its time-traveling tendencies and come into the present moment with your body. Thank your mind for dropping in, being present, and bringing its power and energy with it, energizing this moment. Thank you, thank you, thank you.

Next, bring your awareness to your emotional energy. Your feeling energy is more subtle than your physical energy but not as subtle as your mental energy, it's in between the two. It moves more quickly than your physical body but not as quickly as your mind. It has layers, and at any given time, you have multiple feeling layers occurring. Some may be about what's happening today, others about the future, and others about the past.

Give yourself the room to experience all the different feelings that are currently happening within you. The more you relax and become present, the more your pure feelings will surface. Feelings are energy that want to move. When felt and experienced without judgment, analysis, or management, they expand and move on. Allow yourself to feel these feelings in their essence and purity, whether they're feelings of joy, pain, or somewhere in between. Very good.

Now take a moment to thank your feelings for creating such a rich, textured experience in life. We experience people, our passions, our work and hobbies, art and music, as well as pain and sorrow, the highs and lows of it all through our feelings. Thank you, feelings, for creating such a rich, deep experience in life. Thank you, thank you, thank you.

Lastly, bring your awareness to your most subtle energy, sometimes called your spiritual energy. Spiritual energy is the most subtle energy of our being and it also has layers. Of these layers, I'm going to have you focus on a particular layer of your light made of Totumlux, or total light. This aspect of your light innervates your entire being inside and out, and is always 100% healthy, whole and resonating at your highest potential. It serves as a blueprint or guide for your wellness and the actualization of your soul's purpose and potential.

Visualize and sense this light as it illuminates your entire being, all of your cells, all of your molecules, your DNA. Feel and see this light surrounding you in all directions as it extends to the furthest reaches of your energy field. This beautiful luminous light contains all of your authentic light codes and frequencies that make you unique. It continually blesses you with its presence.

Now, let's connect your light to the light body of the Earth and the Sky. The Earth and the Sky both have their own Totumlux expressions, their light bodies of wholeness and wellness. Terralux, or light of the Earth, is the Earth's signature light made of Totumlux energies. Bring your awareness down, down, down, through the layers of the earth until you reach its center, where you see a big ball of light. This is the earth's blueprint for wholeness and wellness.

See a ray of Terralux rising up, up, up, through the layers of the earth and reaching your body at the base of your spine. It creates a column of light as it goes up through your torso, through your neck, your head, out the top of your head and into the heavens connecting with Aerlux, the light of the Sky. You are now connected to both the Earth and the Sky through a pillar of light that runs through your core.

Feel the Terralux coming from below, and Aerlux, coming from above, moving through you and meeting in the middle, which is your spiritual heart. This is where the energies of the Earth and the Sky meet, creating balance, love, healing, growth, and gratitude. They become the frequencies of compassion and forgiveness. Feel this energy as the music of your heart, Corcanti.

Sometimes it's easier to tangibly experience Corcanti by picturing your loved ones, those you care about deeply and have compassion for. Picture your loved ones before you and as you do, feel what's happening in your heart center. Is there any movement, vibration, subtle pressure, or opening? This is the music of your heartstrings being played, Corcanti.

Corcanti isn't just for others, but for ourselves as well. Now bring this Corcanti around for yourself and wrap yourself in a blanket of it, giving yourself deep self-compassion, self-acceptance, and self-love. Ahh. As you surround yourself with self-gratitude, notice if anything blocks this self-compassion, like self-judgment or feelings of unworthiness. Give these feelings space to be felt and acknowledged but do not believe in them. Let them expand, move on and dissipate, making more room for your self-compassion to go even deeper. This is Autograti. Thank you, thank you, thank you to yourself!

Now that we have awakened and experienced Terralux, the energy rising from the earth, and Aerlux, the energy descending from the sky, along with Corcanti, the frequencies of our heart, and Autograti, our own self-compassion, let's go one step deeper by returning to

Totumlux, the premier light at the source of all these energies.

You are light. Some of this light manifests as your body, mind and feelings, and some of your light is eternal, always shining as your essential whole self. Your manifest self is made of Partiolux, or partial light, always changing and in the process of growing, or dying, or both. Your unmanifest self is pure Totumlux, and your awareness undistracted by thought senses this eternal energy.

Once again, gently ask your mind to relax the time travel, and bring its power and energy into the present moment. There is nothing to do, figure out or create. Simply be, allowing yourself to luxuriate in each breath, your power, the center of your being.

Feel this deep inner balance, inner peace. This experience is Paxlibra, the peace of balance. Become aware of it every day, from the balance of Terralux and Aerlux that flows to you and through you, or the compassion Corcanti and Autogratis that flows from you and for you, or the awareness of Totumlux and Partiolux that makes up all of creation. Paxlibra is knowing the depth and beauty of you as a being of light connected fully in this sea of light. Enjoy the blessings of Paxlibra!

10
DEFINITIONS WITH ROOT WORDS

Aerlux noun: the subtle and gentle light of the air element, representing communication, visionary thinking, intuition, imagination and faith. Roots: aer; Latin for air or atmosphere, lux; Latin for light, radiance

Autogratis verb: surrounding oneself in the Corcanti energy of unconditional love and compassion, accepting both the whole and the broken pieces. Roots: autos; Greek for self or same, gratus; Latin for grateful or pleasing, gratis; Latin for something given or received without any payment required.

Corcanti noun: the transformative light of the spiritual heart, which creates balance, healing and unconditional love, and is created by the meeting of Terralux and Aerlux. Roots: cor; Latin for heart, cantus; Latin for singing or song

Dimentina noun: the complete forgetting of our source light, where we came from before we joined a Partiolux body. Roots: dimentin; Latin for they forget and dimentina; Latin for diminutive.

Microvita noun: small life or the identification with Partiolux, the creative light that breaks down, resulting in a sense of separation from the totality of one's being. Roots; micro; Greek for small, vita; Latin for life.

Partiolux noun: a derivative of Totumlux, the light that creation is made of which is subject to deterioration. Roots: partialis; Latin for divisible, partial, lux; Latin for light, illumination that allows objects to be seen.

Paxlibra verb: Luxuriating in the experience of wholeness coming from the awareness and balance of these light forces in and around you. Roots: pax; Latin for peace, state of tranquility, harmony and absence of conflict. libra; Latin for balance or even

Terralux noun: The grounded and stable light of the earth element, representing stability, manifestation and practicality. Roots: terra: Latin for earth or land, the physical substance of the earth as well as the Earth as a whole, lux; Latin for light, luminosity

Totumlux noun: The unchanging light from which all beings spring. It is the highest frequency of light that encompasses all other frequencies of light. Roots: totum: Latin for whole or all, the entirety of something without any parts excluded, lux: Latin for light, including the spiritual concept of divine light.

ABOUT THE AUTHOR

Raya Alexander's journey is a harmonious fusion of spiritual awakening and worldly achievements. In her 20s, she embarked on a transformative path, residing in a yoga ashram where she delved into profound yoga and meditation practices. Simultaneously, she studied and practiced energy work as well as how to channel wisdom from higher realms for healing.

Later, she pursued higher education, earning a BA from Yale, and embarked on a 12-year tenure in holistic spa management, ultimately achieving her MBA. Throughout this corporate journey, her passion for spiritual healing remained unwavering, deepening through studies in aura photography and energy reading. Driven by a calling to connect with people on a deeper level, she transitioned to teaching and counseling work, using her particular gift of "light listening" to help people connect to their sacred light and inner healing gifts.

For information on recordings by the author and more go to: www.rayaalexander.com

Made in United States
Troutdale, OR
07/18/2024

21349828R00046